HIGH SPEED
THROUGH
SHOALING WATER

Mr Bill Phipps
918 17 St NW
Calgary AB T2N 2E4

HIGH SPEED THROUGH SHOALING WATER

new poems by

TOM WAYMAN

For Dave —
Full speed ahead!
My best
Tom
3/9

HARBOUR PUBLISHING

Harbour Publishing Co. Ltd.
P.O. Box 219
Madeira Park, BC V0N 2H0
www.harbourpublishing.com

Cover design by Anna Comfort
Cover photograph by Tom Freebairn / www.pacificsoftlight.com
Author photograph by Jeremy Addington
Printed and bound in Canada

Harbour Publishing acknowledges financial support from the Government of Canada through the Book Publishing Industry Development Program and the Canada Council for the Arts, and from the Province of British Columbia through the BC Arts Council and the Book Publishing Tax Credit.

THE CANADA COUNCIL | LE CONSEIL DES ARTS
FOR THE ARTS | DU CANADA
SINCE 1957 | DEPUIS 1957

BRITISH
COLUMBIA
ARTS COUNCIL
Supported by the Province of British Columbia

Library and Archives Canada Cataloguing in Publication

Wayman, Tom, 1945–
    High speed through shoaling water / Tom Wayman.

Poems.
ISBN 978-1-55017-401-4

    I. Title.

PS8595.A9H53 2007   C811'.54   C2007-900187-4

CONTENTS

OUTRIDER

GYPSY HIGHWAY

SIXTY

INGUINAL

Three men held me and cut me.
Their little knife was a silver fish
so sharp it sliced open the edges
of a paper I signed.

        May snow
knocked at the door.

              When they were done
agonized colours
spread across my waist where they cut me
and lower, down the tops of my legs:
feverish yellows
and ominous blues, bleak tints
of the skies of hell.

        Snow
was bandaging the day. The blood here
was mine and not mine: fish blood, dark blood, bat blood
seeping, ay!, where they cut me.

           At night
every abandoned pain returned:
behind my ribs at the spine, buried in one shoulder.
My throat issued mottled flames, black smoke.
For the first time, in a dream I was bored:
waiting for a figure to
cease speaking, for someone to exert himself.
The men who cut me
dreamed of new golf shoes whose cleats

penetrated human skin.

                              My skin,
in May, in the silver snow.

HORNET

Pain was a sound
the room filled.

From amid the sagging flowers
by the bed

a grotesque humming insect
that resembled bee or wasp

darted at the wound
to lower its tiny crowbar

into the still-raw opening
and probe.

Scarlet magma
vaulted the plug of the stinger into air.

Now pain
was in pain.

Matter collapsed on itself
as within the gravitational field of a black hole.

All that existed
was enraged light.

When pain wrested free of that condition
to be only pain again

I heard the hornet-like creature
bumbling along the walls of the world.

RECURRENCE

The blade's sharp tip
strikes again under the belly
unrolling a shock wave of
anguish as it pauses,
pivots to cause flat steel
to scrape apart muscle and flesh
—the wide gape thickening with
red

Or the pain can be merely a box
afloat in the dim room: another presence
with the wind outside in the emptied birch,
weight of duvet
on torso and thighs, furnace purr,
dark dream
of snowstorm

WHO

Who left me
alone with the meadow's frosted blades,
shrivelled leaves of the squash,

and café tables
chained to an icy patio railing
until a May I'll never see?

Am I discarded,
the rest gone on? Or am I meant
to herd something forward?

What abandoned me
to watch a stream of mist
hover over the river?

Why does no other isolation
stand at my side
to listen to the whitening of the fields?

THE FOUNTAIN

When dusk began to fill the valleys'
declivities and
gullies, I was drawn to an opening
through the spruce and fir
—the path to the fountain
at which my parents drank and vanished.
At that creek, I am told, the water ripples
dark to those visitors enshrouded by
rage, by gloom
or blue to others
of a calmer mind
or translucent: revealing the rocks
the stream tumbles and
eddies over. The sound
in the thickening light
is the muted pulses
of a heart. Where a person kneels
at the little bay, the pebbles
are worn small
as sand, as ash.
Water lifted to the lips
dissolves the swallower into water
or air. Beyond this bank
the flow pours down bearing
snowmelt, bearing specks of earth,
bearing supple twigs or
sere leaves
—heedless of who drinks
or who has not yet heard
of this course
or who now approaches
its fatal shore.

HIGH SPEED THROUGH SHOALING WATER

Some hours, even days, I flew above that country
not confined by any device
but with air streaming over my arms
and face, while another wind
uttered a spray of leaves
into the air—if that was the season—
or a float of cottonseeds
along the river.

                As I banked, weaved through the valley
between stands and hillsides of
larch and pine and fir,
veered past cliffs, or birch and alder tops
below in the old cutblocks and watercourses,
while beside the road, power and telephone lines
precipitated, raced from pole to pole, and evaporated,
I admit that fear
flowed amid the exhilaration
—if I sailed too close to the forest crown,
or when I crested a ridge I hadn't perceived
and the woods without warning instantly descended
hundreds of metres, the vast drop underneath
swelling the pull of gravity
so in a terrifying lurch I seemed tugged
down, but corrected for it

                      and soared on: a wing of air
passing through air
sun-driven, that angled toward an approaching
white-capped
range of stone.

UNDER

When I wished to slip below ground,
stretch out horizontal, and drift to sleep,
I found the spot crowded
and busier than I imagined.
I'd no sooner pulled the sod
above my hair
than I found my legs difficult to extend
due to a mesh of roots
—some thick, gnarled, others more wire-like
but exhibiting great tensile strength.
And the texture of the subsoil
was uneven: pockets were soft loam,
yet other areas mainly gravel,
arduous to shift aside.
Rocks were peppered across the space, too,
most fist-sized or smaller,
a few larger than my head
but each wedged tightly into earth.
Plus the locale
was densely inhabited:
microbial organisms, worms, voles
picked their way through the region.
"You're too big,"
an armoured beetle complained.
"A boulder large as you
would displace the rest of us. Why not settle elsewhere?"
I only want to dream,
I replied. *The moment I'm asleep*
I'll vanish from here.
"No time for rest," the insect countered.
"Inches yet to cover.
Everything there is to do."

ALPS ALTURAS: SIXTY

On a scree slope in the Goat Range
my boots spool a trail rock by rock
into the first decade of my life
I dread the finish of. At the start
I climbed through dense conifers and brush
gradually thinning to subalpine
meadows, August-scattered with Indian paintbrush,
aster, even late-flowering lupine
amid islands of diminutive spires of fir
and Engelmann spruce, the open places among the ridges
traversed by small creeks
and by stone beds of runoff watercourses,
dry at this season. I and my companions
descended, crossed, switchbacked up from
these angled fields
with eyes constantly scrutinizing the hillsides, our party
shouting and talking so as not to startle the unseen
powers, our blown whistles
occasionally answered by a pika's squeak,
a marmot's echo.

The day
plodded up through cols
and along ridges, until I cleared the treeline, my pack
heavier with each rise, worked around a massive boulder
and out onto scree.

Far down the rockslide
beneath my legs, a miniature canyon
proffers spoon tarns, sustained from the threads of
waterfalls on the face of Mount Inverness
opposite my perch. To the northern, eastern, southern

distances, range beyond range retreats
into lightening tones of blue.

                              But my route leads
a different way: my body, sturdy with a long summer's
tasks and pleasures,
hoists my feet and swings them. No place to turn
on this track
that bears me stone by stone
toward a snow-locked lake, around whose shore
nothing is made by hands.

WIND CAROL: THE SOUND

I am going to vanish entirely,
to have never existed. Not a trace
of my days on earth
will vibrate.
Who recalls a single detail
of my mother's mother
or of Mrs. Jmaeff down the lane,
of my great-uncle Herschel's father?

With me is lost
the tangible pressure of hot July sunlight
on my chest and face.
How my bared feet trod on
silvery pebbles of water
when I crossed grass newly soaked by the hose.

And a cooling river of air
downridge on a summer's evening
that oddly also carries puffs of heat.

Nobody will know I loved the sough of wind
in the uppermost branches
more than the chords and rhythms of music,
more than even words. I heard a wisdom
other than human
flow through the gravely swaying limbs
of the spruce
or the leafed birch, the sound
of another way of being

in this world: at once
solemn, practical, austere.

The breeze rises
and the poplars speak,
then are silent.
In time these trunks
will fall to earth
or be cut down.
But the wind, for as long as
the trees abide,
will live forever.

HOW AM I DOING FOR TIME?

I

At a dinner, I encounter somebody
I haven't seen in several years. Decades before
he and his wife were part of that group of friends
I considered most important to my life.
What intervenes
to demote a person from that role?
Too much geography? Too much family? A challenging job
or the search for one? I stare at him
across the table. He has jowls now;
his hair, nearly white, has retreated far up his forehead.
He looks exactly how I remember his father.

The bodies of everyone about my age
are thickening, loosening, giving way.
Frequently I think my peers have *decided*
to look older, a fashion choice
like how forty years ago each of us
showed up in flared jeans, then sometime later
adopted straight legs again.
Now, after a few minutes' conversation,
these people's lively natures
fog out the folds and creases on their faces,
their grey, evaporating hair, the details
of their latest encounter with modern medicine.
Yet every person is more private,
less engaged with the rest of us. The adventures we shared
have become experiences we no longer expect
even our fellow participants to truly comprehend.

II

When my mother was dying, her grocery list, incomplete,
lay on the kitchen counter by the toaster.
The final occasion I remember her out of bed
she was hunched in her dressing gown over the slip of paper
adding an item or two. But she
was no longer doing the shopping. A different column of nouns
fuelled the household's voyage through the weeks.

After my father's memorial service,
among the sheaves of papers on his desk was
the inventory of chores he'd outlined to accomplish
when he returned from the operation on his leg:
bank deposit, dry cleaners, clarinet reeds.
Yet an alternate set of obligations
was determined for him,
and then for his body. The scribbled tasks
rested face-up, waiting forever
for a pen to be struck through the letters.

III

I like the light.
In the country, I joke that
the dark belongs to the animals: the bears that pass by the house
fall and spring, leaving their mounds of scat
for me to view in the morning. Or if I'm ever on some urgent errand
after nightfall to or from the truck,
deer occasionally shock me with the sudden pulse of their hoofbeats
retreating. Following sunset
I stay indoors
unless checking the stars from the deck.

I like the light.
In the country, I love to nap of an afternoon on the couch
and gaze through the window up at the huge firs and pines
west of the house, that will outlast me,
or at the white and blue sky
with its shifting configurations
that will outlast me. How pleasant to wake
to the wind moving the cedar branches
and the tongues of the wind chimes.
In blackness, my dreams
most often are stressful, menacing.

I will spend a very long time
in the dark
without a face
or word.

Only the light
knows my name.

ETERNAL

Two crows
lift from the flank of a half-frozen deer

lying coated with sand
in the April ditch

Ragged wisps of cloud
trail down from the blanked-out summit ridge

—snowfall on the peaks
The road through the valley

edges a lake
whose ice sheet has pulled back from the shore

Whether I once lived
a raven flaps off a twiggy branch

beside the asphalt
and glides up to settle on a spruce limb

across the rock cut
The baby's head—soaked black hair—

crowns
as hands reach to receive it

Traffic sparse; by late afternoon
rain on the mountain

GREENUP

When the switch trips, and I convert
to nothing
a small swath will open in space-time as on a hillside
someone clears a mature stand of cedar
beside a dirt road far in along a creek
or, in a front valley, a landowner empties
an acre or two of mixed spruce and pine above his house

Neighbours notice, of course, and frequent visitors
to the vicinity, but otherwise the stripped area
with its litter of branch detritus, burn piles and churned brown earth
stares vacantly up at the stars and rain

Next spring, however, tufts of coarse grasses
break the surface, then bracken
and inch-high shoots of alder and hazel scrub
Chill gusts of snow
shrivel these eventually
But when May recycles, the green lifts higher
as this scrape fills in: dense with
thimbleberry brush, baby firs and
larches, the first coloured column of lupine

Newcomers to the region assume
that the patch is an old fire scar
or that rock just below the humus
accounts for the lack of tree cover
After decades, though, only an expert could speculate
once the woods close over entirely
that an absence existed here
And nobody would have a reason
to employ such a vegetative archaeologist

since with the disappearance of memory
the universe attains perfection
—two crows complain as they oar above the forest
about an osprey downriver
The June day
hovers on the sun-dazed ridge

PORTRAIT OF MYSELF
AS A CLOUD

SPRINGBOMB

Alder, birch, mountain ash detonate
on the hills or alongside the roads.
Each explosion generates green clouds
that feather away at the edges.
These blasts trigger hazel and larch,
merge with the continuous eruption
of the ridges' fir, hemlock, pine
until the valley resounds
with an incessant green concussive roar.

A BIRD MADE OF LIGHT

June leaves of the alder and hazel thicket
between the house and the forested mountain
shimmer in wave on wave of
luminous sulphur-lime.
All morning, submerged far in the dark earth,
their roots tug along intertwined threads
nutrients deposited when the stones and loam
were lakeshore or valley bottom.
These black particles,
lifted through trunk and branch and twig,
are transformed to untainted
light, which each tree
exhales through ten thousand leaves,
pumping the radiance aloft
hour after hour,
pulsing a green brilliance back toward the sun.

And in the charged medium rippling upwards
hangs the single shrill note of the flicker,
the cries of darting chickadee,
of the clumsier Steller's jay, robin
and a disturbance of crows that thrash through
the tops of the pines and firs
or that coast overhead

where the brightness that evaporates from the foliage
bears the beaks' sounds higher
to shape in the pinnacle of the sky
a bird
made of light.

WIND CAROL: ASPEN

Aspen are always eager
to generate a wind.
They continually urge
other trees to participate,
jingling leaves and branches,
taunting *C'mon. Don't be so conservative.*
Let's get a gale happening.
Wasn't it fun last time?

The aspen's delinquent plea
occasionally wins over
the serious cedars, who begin to
flap ponderous limbs
higher and lower, slowly,
like bellows.
Hemlock and spruce
join, increasing the pace, then the birch
and maple until
everywhere trunks and leaves,
frenzied, toss and
churn, whip and bend,
to the aspen's manic delight.

POST

Earth does not like things forced into it.
Hyacinth or a spruce seedling or onions
climb between pebbles and through grains of soil
and pass into air with the ground's blessing.
Yet a wooden fence post stuck into the meadow
is no sooner tamped into position than it feels
the earth's teeth start to gnaw on its skin.

When the post eventually topples,
it will have sheared off
precisely at the boundary between light and dark
—as though the soil declared:
You keep what belongs to you.
I'll do the same.
Thus the portion that has supported wire
or wooden rails is relatively intact.
But if someone digs
to excavate the remnant under the surface,
the post below the jagged break has shrunk,
been partially digested—
transformed to a substance useful among the stones.

Earth seems to regard its emissaries
as vital to good relations between
clay and air: the ground readily issues permits
for its citizens to cross the frontier.
But if not made of cement, even house foundations
suffer the fate of fences.
Indeed, as soon as concrete is poured and cures,
dirt's ally, water, attempts to end the invasion,
to vanquish what has descended into loam's territories.

Of course, we creatures of the upper world
behave to an extent like the ground:
cutting off some grasses and certain trees and flowers
just where they intrude into the weather.
Yet most travellers from underneath we leave untouched,
while every substance we insert into soil
is surrounded, assaulted, and vanishes
as if placed in fire.

NOCTURNE

A full moon
is describing the hazels' leaves and branches
as featureless cascades of
pure light, the tall pines and firs
it has lifted over
as stiff black board.
The moon has no word
for dark, for the shadowed lawns'
ominous calm. The moon ignores
the things it cannot enunciate,
while its fervent language drowns out
the exclamations of the stars.

PORTRAIT OF MYSELF AS A CLOUD,
OR NATURAL FEATURE ON THE VALLEY FLOOR

Sixteen years now
Jerome Creek
has been drawn down my throat
—the water flowing into
a diversion pipe, across
Cowern's woods to
the distribution box,
burbling into the southernmost of
ten compartments, the one
I share with three other
households, then along a half-mile
or more of line
to my kitchen faucet. Season upon season
the Creek suffuses through my stomach
and other organs
and out to my skin: is excreted
or evaporated
while I bury garlic cloves
in late October, clear the drifts
from the bend in my long driveway,
prune apple and plum
in a fine March mist. The discarded liquid
that soaks into my septic field
or lifts into the Valley sky
causes my existence here
to resemble each permanently temporary
pond or water meadow
or stretch of River course. The fluid I release
to ground, to air
is borne away in the vast ocean of the winds

or under the earth
but at last reaches the salt sea.

There, the substance is transmuted
back to its pure form
and carried by the storm track
eastward across the Coast Range
and the Monashees
to sift down as snow
high on Perry Ridge,
as rain on the forested
catchment north of Richards's
and south of Avis's drainages, seeping and
trickling into minuscule tributaries,
then tumbling down as white spray and
hasty motion
to the inlet pipe
and to me, itinerant and rooted
in this Valley as any cumulonimbus
lumbering overhead, as the deking flocks of
waxwings in the week or two
the red mountain ash berries are ripest,
as the June rise, as weather
—the stream pouring through me,
that I am part of,
making my name as much Jerome Creek
as any other appellation.

SECRETS OF SUMMER

i

Hands of birch leaves, maple
pat the warm air

ii

Repositioning the irrigation sprinkler
after it pulsed a circle for an hour
I enter
a dome of coolness
between the lawn's damp floor
spruce and hazel walls

iii

An immense dark cloud
the size of the Valley
bulges over a mountain rim
and above me

Only the sky
is vaster

iv

Fresh-mowed hay's
scent of sugary chlorophyll

On the tongue, its taste
would be filaments of
cotton candy

Each May, a distinct *fizz*
sounds in the green woods' silence
—an electric sizzling
or hose water that strikes leaves
of the aspen or
white-flowered thimbleberry

In summer stillness
a low
hum exhales
from the hot ground

Three-quarters-full July moon
drenches the bed
through the open east window

When I wake, the sheets are soaked by
heat: the sun
has summited the day's
first mountain

BEAR BALLAD

Stunted spruce watched me
climb in the slanted light.
The meadow was pitched
steeper than a roof.

I placed a foot
buried to the shin in leaves of
ferns, asters, hellebores,
and slipped back, slipped back,

stepped again. My eyes
scanned the tilted field
in the tilted light
to the rocky summit for what rises

out of the ground
or between the twisted stems of the conifers
downslope, where the woods pant and collapse
unable to ascend farther:

black fur
with its hump and white teeth
—the dam and her cubs, the sire
with his pig nose of oblivion.

In the story, the hunters find skins and fur
draped over bushes beside a tarn
where pink flesh splashes in the water.
If they can steal these coats

they live, are absorbed into the death they wear.
My father in his fur, my mother

in hers. My uncle Alex. Dennis Wheeler.
And the roaring boys: Dave Forsyth, sailor,

Dave Bostock,
welder and singer. Joan Partridge,
Bron Wallace, Shelley Weyland.
"Nothing to it," they cry or growl,

flaunt their dark garment.
My ears, that hear them,
cooled in that afternoon sun.
My eyes swept and swept the descending field.

NOCTURNE II

A siren threads north: red flash
a mile across the Valley
pursued by the high percussive wailing of dogs.

Above the eastern ridge
burn the tiny cauldrons of time
speckled in their galaxies toward the zenith.

When I go, among what I will regret
are the stars.

SHIFT

On a hot August morning,
a few leaves of the dogbane
—the knee-high undergrowth
that clusters along the road
and across the slopes closest to my house—
have yellowed. Next day
a few more have changed. Now I notice
the grasses of my neighbours' fields
are as much brown as green.

Then some leaves on the young birches
and in the crowns of older aspens
and among the bracken
have lightened. The tasselled corn
continues to drive its spikes higher into air,
the tight knot of every plum
loosens a little each day,
the apples flush with the effort
of expanding in such heat.
The mountainside
is redolent with pine
and the spices of the forest floor.
Squirrels, though, are suddenly noisy
in the hazels, and flocks of nuthatch,
waxwing, flicker
work the wood's edge
and the lawn's maple and alder. The heavy sun
continues to shrink the river.
But another mood has entered the Valley
through the light-choked afternoon.
Everything that lives can taste a different season
in green gone stale in groves and pastures,

in the tarnished gold flaring
across cutbanks and by ditches,
in the cooler shadow when a cloud
pushes between the summer and the sky.

THE PEOPLE WHO USED TO OWN THIS PLACE

The May piglets who frisk around the sty,
pleased to bump each other and dash apart,
are transformed in a season to huge somnolent porkers
that lumber only toward feed
when they reluctantly hoist themselves to their hooves.

We each count our summers
in this Valley: our brief portion
of the eons these forested mountains
ringed a lake that formerly beached
high on what are now ridges.
Descending benches along the slopes
mark the successive centuries where the waters paused
before they drained away to the meandering river
followed here by the first whites
—whose downstream dams
block the Kokanee from spawning
and thus purify the river to
a sterile vessel that travels steadily past
homestead, bungalow, clear-cut acreage.

We empty out of the Valley ourselves:
our memorial the structures we build,
the reconfigurations of the hillsides
and meadows we contract for
or borrow a friend's tracked excavator
for a weekend to effect,
our epitaph the complaints or praise of
whoever next possesses our titles, water licences,
gardens: truest heirs in all but name
of our breath, our labour, our Septembers.

AUTUMN SECRETS

i

On the margins of field and road
low dogbane foliage

speckled as much yellow as green
reprises June's sun-dapple

ii

Each morning
the light cooler
shrunken

iii

Tomato and pepper stalks, branches
emptied of fruit
purposeless

Arugula become stringy shoots, its remaining leaves
bitter
The basil dry, tasteless

Rows of carrot and onion tops
vanished
Butternut squashes not large enough to pick
clinging to stems
tense with apprehension about
frost

iv

Weeds erupt across the garden
—summer's dishevelled grave

v

In the woods and lanes
gilded and amber scatterlings of
the birch, alder
The larches' furred lace
dusted orange

vi

An aspen flake
flutters down
—grey-white bird that angles low
settling onto earth

as hazel, cottonwood leaves
swirl out in a cascade or
riffle
—a closing chord's
dying fall

AUTUMN HEAT

The sun is pressure-blasting
the pavement white

                            as my eager vehicle follows
the road, a hand ghosting
a polished tabletop, caressing the rounds
of lathed wood, fingers that delight in
an unimpeded drift across skin, over ribs,
ecstatic weighing of
a breast's syncline and anticline

September sun
is bleaching the pavement

                            —that light sweet as thigh flesh
with its uplands and
dim moist swale
while mulleins erect beside the highway
impatiently push through foliage toward

sun that scalds
asphalt white

                     The hot spray, the road
are both fecund and
fatal incubators
that offer birth to miles, to
woods, river, the ambulance's crown of
flashing lamps, a route
that twists upward to a crest where

the sun is staining
the pavement white

                        —a brush
sweeping across the
afternoon
—gorged, urgent, ardent

GROVE

A grove of high firs,
limbs weighted with snow:
the trees a cluster of dignified parents
watching a gathering of children
—their own, and the town's.
The parenting techniques these adults practise
involve silence and patience,
the communication of neither approval nor distaste
at what their progeny yell or play with
or wreck, at how the youngsters interact
and with whom. These grown-ups aim
to model decent conduct
rather than intervene constantly to
correct or reward. Like all parents,
these can be hurt
or ignored or mocked
by their squabbling, thoughtless
offspring. But the very height
and quietude of these trees
distinguishes them from
the beings
they remotely, respectfully
wish to raise
to a larger life.

SECRETS OF WINTER

i

A coyote's cry at 3 a.m.
loud enough to be close
under my window.
Nothing in the snowlit meadow.

ii

Canada geese settle on a neighbour's field
day after day: suddenly the small flock
ascends toward the river,
just clearing the pine and leafless cottonwood
before their return. They poise
on the snow. After many minutes,
a head shifts.

iii

Last summer's eagle
banks against clouds
above the bridge that takes the back road
out to the highway.
The bird alights in a white-tipped fir
and disappears.
The treetop shakes, heavy wings
impel themselves aloft into the thermals.

iv

Indentations of deer hooves
stitch the drifts covering the lawn
and intersect two paths I shovel
house to compost pile, house to driveway.
Tracks also mark these routes of mine
for a brief distance.

v

Waxwing or woodpecker
pumps and darts
between the cedars' boughs
and the pines', strains toward
a gate into the dark woods.

vi

The pavement follows a bench
high over a river valley.
Snow on the wind pours up
out of a draw.

EMBLEM

A bright March morning, snow deep
on the roofs and meadows of the Valley floor.
But dull brown gaps widen each afternoon
in tree wells, and down the edges of roads and lanes.

The ridgelines aloft are solid white
as are the upper reaches of the forest that descends
toward the white fields that border the river.
In the strengthening sunshine, Frog Mountain's summit

—a sugarloaf of snow—
soars over the visible ranges. And alongside this peak,
floating in a sky blue as summer
the moon's round ghost is five days past full

but transparent—airy spirit
of this between-season, holed ensign
hoisted defiant above a besieged capital
asserting for the final time its bone-cold reign.

OUTRIDER

THE STONE

The boss advances toward me across the room.
Before I can focus on his intent
he slams a huge stone into my stomach
and grinds it in.
I can scarcely breathe.
Through my pain and its weight,
he speaks.
As I try to inhale, exhale,
instead of hearing anything I watch a silvery fluid,
viscous and lumpy,
waterfall over his lower lip
and shower onto the stone,
spraying my shirt and trousers.

Then the boss has vanished
but the boulder remains jammed into my abdomen.
I feel a tug on each arm
and two colleagues propel me forward.
I stumble step after step,
half-bent over the embedded mass of rock.
My guides lead me down a familiar hallway
to the main entrance.
They, too, are talking
yet in my dizziness their utterances
appear a diluted version
of words the boss said. The liquid this time
splatters over the corridor's linoleum
and across their shoes and mine.

I lean against the railing of
the front stairs outside, alone.
Acres of parked vehicles

wink and glisten in the light.
I do not understand how I could drive
with this stone protruding from my torso,
nor how to discover which buses
I require in place of my car
or where to locate the number for a taxi.
The stone, slick with moisture,
throbs relentlessly in my belly.
I lower myself in careful stages to sit on the cement.
I know I cannot walk
as far as I need to go.

IN THE DUMPER

"Always take a crap on the company nickel,"
was his advice. "Figure we make, what,
sixteen an hour including benefits?
That means a four-dollar shit
at least. Plus, bring a paper
'cause you want to keep on top of
the news, how the military everyplace around the world
are exporting democracy and freedom.
Gotta time your stay, though,
to finish before the foreman shows up, orders you
back to your machine."

CARROT

For years I dwelt in an apartment
whose window gazed at a bridge across Burrard Inlet
over which traffic at every hour rose toward downtown
or returned, while the hours themselves
flashed from a distant neon sign, so I had everything
I could want: youth and time and the sea

In my third-floor room I was happy
with the typewriter I returned to each day after clocking out
with friends scattered throughout this building
as well as people I scarcely knew: the couple through the south wall
whose fights and unhappy love
leaked in nights above the steady rain against my window
Or beautiful Kathy one floor below
I occasionally had to phone at two in the morning
to ask her to quiet down a party

In those days
I was aware five thousand dollars
would provide my needs for a year
And since interest
drew easily ten per cent
all I had to save was fifty thousand
to recline at my ease forever
hunched over the keys of my typewriter
filling the dwelling around me and the street outside
where the cars raced down to the beach
with my words

This was the carrot
I have pursued my entire life
Each time I approached, inflation

meant the sum I had calculated as sufficient
now could provide only half a year
of existence, then a quarter
Next, after I readjusted my figures
interest rates began to plummet
so the amount I needed to amass
distended exponentially

                          Decade upon decade
the carrot has swung before me
from a pole hoisted aloft by fleering faces
who adroitly step back whenever I lunge
or shuffle closer to the suspended vegetable

                                        Nor have the years been kinder
to the carrot
Even as it blurs
in its incessant wavering motion
its desiccated status is evident
by its flaccid greenery, ever-more-pallid colour
I believe that only once it retains absolutely no food value
will I be permitted to clutch it
in a withered fist

                    Far better to have joined
with my friends and successfully planted
our own seeds, to have raised
a different crop
Though we worked to this end
we failed to organize a different arrangement
than to have a dying succulence
constantly dangled just ahead, while the tide
advances and falls, the dollars swell
nearer the required line

and recede, the traffic
climbs each morning toward the sky

BALLAD OF THE PICKUPS

The favourite vehicle of multimillionaires
According to one survey
Is the Ford F-Series pickup truck:
Such owners adopting the guise

Of the majority who steer out every morning
To the jobsite, or employee parking lot
—Those of us sheltered paycheque to paycheque
Only by our debts from the term

"Indigent." This automotive predilection
Of the wealthy is hardly a surprise
Given that the religion of many of them
Worships a poor man

Amid sumptuous surroundings
In which the virtues of poverty
Are lauded by clerics on a guaranteed income
Who tend their sheep

With a golden shepherd's crook,
Dexterously escorting a flock of
Late-model pickups
Through the eye of a needle.

ANTHEM

They say we're built to take it.
Our work earns one-third
to one-hundredth the annual cheques of a company executive
because, they insist, otherwise the business
couldn't attract a strong management team
and because leadership bonuses are necessary
to provide incentive to excel.
We joke: "The further away from actually producing
goods and services, the more money you receive." We kid:
"The less you're paid, the worse you're treated."
Yet we don't complain;
we're built to take it.

They say we're built to take it.
As customers, it's okay if we wait in line as long as they please
since their sole alternative would be to hire more of us
which wouldn't be in the best interest of the shareholders
and thus ultimately, they explain,
of consumers. And if the enterprise falters,
it's perfectly reasonable that the president and vice-presidents
whose decisions resulted in the financial collapse
should depart with a few million to ease their transition
to another position of responsibility
while we get a month's severance
if the union can swing it. And should the pension
we've had deducted each month for twenty-seven years
vanish along with the outfit, while the bosses
in the last days were cashing in their stock options
to secure their own financial future, well,
no problem because
we're built to take it.

In addition, they tell us: "*We*'re built to take it."
They mean that some people, like them, possess
the smarts and the energy and the drive
while others like us are just born to serve,
to be followers. They argue: "Our hard work
should be rewarded, whereas your hard work
would be impossible without our hard work,
so *naturally* we should receive more.
If we have to fudge the books a trifle
or grease a few palms to obtain subsidies
out of your tax money, while steadily preaching
the virtues of free enterprise
in a free market, hey, that's a component of risk.
If there's anything we are, it's risk-takers.
Pay no attention to the termination agreements
in the executive contracts, or to the limited liability clauses
the law allows, or to the insurance industry,
or to the *re*-insurance industry. We thrive on risk,
and risk ought to be rewarded.
Too bad if you didn't get your share.
But, as we mentioned, we're built to take it."

I, too, would say *We're built to take it.*
My perspective, though, is rather along the lines of
the factory adage: "If you can run that machine,
you can wreck it." I'd argue
since we make it all, we can take it all.
Planning, coordination, staffing are only functions
as vital as every other facet of the enterprise.
If the owner can create product
by himself or herself, that's fine.
But if he or she has to hire even one of us
then *two* people are turning this wheel.
Who arranged that return on investment

should include, besides cash,
unelected authority over other people?
In the great push of history, more freedom
for more of the population
is the most tenacious fad. Back when there were peasants,
serfs, the landowners screeched plenty about
their inherent right to rule, not to mention
God's personal approval of the existing chain of command.
Eventually, those on the bottom of this pyramid
kicked it over, called themselves farmers and citizens, and,
at least for a while in various places around this sweat-stained globe,
seized the soil they ploughed and planted. What happened subsequently
is another story
or maybe an object lesson. But I maintain
we're overdue for acquiring our part
in running things. Who better than us
knows every problem and success on the line,
which hoses are due for replacement,
who's a slacker, what aspects of Standard Procedure result in
shoddy output, whether there really are benefits
in subcontracting to the superintendent's brother-in-law?
Sooner or later, even this place has to be democratic.
That urge toward freedom seems almost
genetic, which is why I claim: we're built
to take it.

AUDIENCE

The chairs in this auditorium are attentive,
unfailingly ready to listen, though too shy
to ever ask a question. They face front, don't fidget.
Their obliging nature is evident
in how they patiently bear the weight of people
who file in occasionally and sit atop them
—the girth of some of these men and women
representing a strain to support.
Yet no protest is offered either as the newcomers
block the chairs' view of the speaker,
if a coat has not already been tossed over the backrest,
completely blinding them.

When the talk or performance is finished,
the human beings amble out
leaving the assembly of chairs, once the lights are killed,
alone in the room in orderly rows.
Anybody glancing in would be offered
the picture of loyal obedience.

Except when the chairs are certain no person is around
suddenly one of them breaks the silence by declaring:
"*That* sure sucked." The other chairs
burst out laughing. Then one of the more juvenile of those here
maybe will make a farting noise
or a different one a lewd comment.
A chair utters some observation
audible only to those nearest it in the southeast corner
who howl uproariously

while across the room others inquire:
"What did she say?"

But none wait for the answer.
Conversations erupt everyplace
as the words the chairs were recently subjected to from the podium
are forgotten. All present return to consider
their own gossip
and rumours, the issues
important to chairs.

TEACHING ENGLISH

What does English not know
that it needs to hear from me? So many instructors
have drawn its attention to the absurd spelling,
how chopping a tree down
is not the opposite of chopping a tree up.
The language has endured enough talk
about the "they're"/"their"/"there" wackiness
and users' continual bafflement
over the purpose of the apostrophe.

Can I convey anything
to help English function better
where it earns a paycheque
or during intimate encounters?
I regard it, scratch my head.
It stares back at me while it sits,
headphones on, earbuds pumping music
directly into the auditory nerve,
vocabulary shrinking along with
cognitive ability—consequence of too much television
before age three, perhaps, or excessive cellphone use
—eyes blank
as a missing comma.

DEATH OF THE GRANDMOTHERS

Week ten of the fourteen-week
semester: the Regional Health Authority
issues its standard internal Bulletin
for this time of year. In accordance with
policy, Emergency Rooms are instructed
to immediately implement Disaster Plan procedures
including an increase in staff, designation of extra beds,
and a denial of all leave and vacation requests.
In what the Bulletin describes as
"an unpleasant but sadly necessary
aspect of our duties," local funeral homes are alerted
for an influx of clients.

                    The Bulletin specifies that
most at risk at this juncture are the elderly
—especially, for reasons not clear,
grandmothers.

            In educational institutions
across the district, class by class
term papers fall due. Immediately the sirens and pulsing lights of ambulances
choke the avenues, inside nursing-home wards
crash carts are propelled down hallways
by frantic cardiac arrest teams. Despite the cyclical predictability
of this epidemic, the dollars allotted to
research, prevention and preparedness,
hearse after hearse backs into the rear loading bays
of clinics, or into the driveways of apartment buildings
and private houses.

            So as not to alarm
the general population, the demise of so many grandmothers

is kept not only from newspapers and evening broadcasts
but even from the obituary pages.
Every so often a member of the area Health Board
will state—off the record of course—he or she believes
the existing protocol is wrong,
that a public Medical Advisory should be declared
the first day handouts bearing term essay topics
are distributed. Yet to date the opinion of the Board's majority
holds sway, and twice a year
health care providers must brace for
a steep increase in death watch upon death watch,
each with its concomitant funeral,
a contagion that flares and then subsides
only when the district's final overdue assignment
is slipped beneath an instructor's door.

POSTMODERN 911

The speaker at the podium is in the midst of rattling off quotes
from several critical theorists as definitive proof
that neither language nor history permit
definitive statements or authorities.
I leap from my seat and stride forward.
As I approach he turns toward me, face puzzled
above his lecture notes
so I hit him twice in the mouth.
His papers fly off the lectern. Uproar in the audience
though nobody utters anything coherent. My hand hurts.
"What are you doing?" he manages, having stepped back a couple of paces,
fingers tenderly feeling his jaw. "Are you completely
nuts?"

       I let him have it in the gut: *doosh doosh.*
When he quits gasping, where he thrashes around on the floor,
I bend over him. "Here's my cellphone. Likely you'll want to call the cops.
I know you just told us reality is strictly a function
of the beholder. But I bet you and I agree
this cellphone is real."

       He glares up at me.
I tap in the famous numbers, proffer the device again
which he snatches. I've activated the speakerphone function
so both sides are audible.

    "Postmodern 911."

"I've been physically attacked by a lunatic, and need help immediately.
I'm in lecture room ST 407, which is—"

"You mean you *believe* you've been attacked.
Truth, you'll be interested to learn, is entirely relative.
The consequences of such relativity are manifold, including—"

"No, damn it, a moron came right out of the audience
and smacked me for no good reason. He—"

"Now, I'm sure there are competing narratives."
The tone via the speaker sounds bored.
"Multiple interpretations of any construct or happening, however,
enormously enrich the human experience.
Of course, if you can legitimately define yourself
as colonized, discriminated against, or
identified as Other with respect to—"

"You don't understand.
This prick came out of nowhere and—"

"Ah, to *you* his origins may constitute 'nowhere',
as you so smugly refer to it. Perhaps his actions,
if such actually occurred, constitute
a trope of tangibly, as it were, writing back to—"

"Metaphor has nothing to do with it.
I've been assaulted. I demand—"

"Your characterization of experience is far too linear.
Listen to the following text, and I'm sure
you'll find its non-narrative structure and accretive compositional strategy
will problematize your description of events and force you
to more accurately comprehend your situation:
Yellow plastic kettles of the environment
condense Bakhtinian anti-logic pliers into—"

"The *police*. Get me the fucking *police*.
This asshole is trying to kill me."

    "I'm afraid reality is more ambiguous
    than postulated by your gendered, probably homophobic,
    probably logocentric world view. See—"

I duck as he throws the cellphone at my head,
scrambles to his feet and adopts a defensive stance:
fists up, fear in his eyes. I consider decking him once more,
when a man wearing a tie appears at my elbow,
the scholar who introduced today's talk.
"That's really all the time we have for this,"
the new arrival proposes in a timorous voice.
To his surprise I nod,
shake him by the hand.

BACKPACK

Lines of young people
ceaselessly shuffle toward a campus across an overpass,
each trudger fitted with a backpack
bulged out by the strain of its contents.
At the bus stops outside the high school, too,
or along the street at every hour
young men and women tow the strapped sacks
into shops, parks, stadiums, movie theatres,
restaurants.

       Streams and clumps of backpacks
pace each thoroughfare
like an army on a forced march
or a train of burdened sherpas. At night someplace,
the pack is lowered onto a chair
or floor, positioned to be hoisted
and reattached to a torso
at dawn.

       What is stuffed
in these bags, that the owners are not permitted
or do not permit themselves
to be absent from? A door
behind which parents
or a parent and step-parent
shouted at one another? A toy elephant, now frayed,
they carried every second weekend
to a different house or apartment? A situation
that cannot be rectified, that you only can be
distracted from

by purchases that thereafter perpetually
must be borne?

              Through decades, these knapsacks
are hauled block after block, destination to destination,
city after city. Do those who transport the packs wonder
how it would feel to cut the buckled strips, discard
their cargo? Yet if they gaze around,
only others saddled like themselves
are visible. Perhaps they nevertheless dream of
floating free of the inventory within, including devices
that hold a thousand songs
the owners never sing, other than to mouth the lyrics for a moment
prompted by the voice of a millionaire or millionairess.
Or maybe they are resigned to drudge forward
under the packs their entire lives:
hard-hat divers whose weights
allow them to ponderously wade through the silt
on the ocean floor, kept alive by lines that pass down to them,
out of a place not visible through the turbidity of the water,
air drawn from a clear and open sky.

MESSAGES

This number is busy
—is involved, at the moment, in too many projects
to talk to you

This number is not in service
It retired last May, and since then
has moved to Tucson, taken up golf seriously
and is constructing an outboard motor from a kit

This number is weirdly dressed
in pajamas, underwear and a beret
Such attire is of course not permitted in the office
although modern technology allows some numbers
—including this one—to function from home

This number is unpredictable
Your call will be routed if these digits feel like it
but past results are no guarantee of future performance

This number is surly and unpleasant
Either you did something to offend it in the past
or else emotional problems or substance abuse
presently are negatively impacting its behaviour

This number believes that you as the consumer
are entirely at fault
if you are bothering it to complain about anything

This number advises you to contact your elected representative
if for any reason you are still not satisfied

MEMORIES OF THE GLACIER

I was raised in the perpetual freezing wind
off the immense Glacier, the ice sheet
larger than several European countries,
with a thickness and weight
many times that of the Andes.
For decades, no one was certain if the Glacier
was in advance or retreat. Each shift—even in millimetres—
in either direction resulted in dozens of news stories
and scientific analyses.
When the Glacier indisputably began to withdraw,
everybody was astounded at the speed of its melt.
What had been an eternal presence, a vast continent-sized refrigerant,
rapidly ceased to occupy the territory
it had stilled.

People almost immediately
wandered into the odd landscape
of the Glacier's previous domination—first singly, then
in groups of settlers
intending to revivify the farms, hamlets, cities
broken under the mass of ice.
Commercial ventures, including resource extraction firms,
also established themselves.

Yet both in newly-open areas
and parts of the globe that have always been ice-free
the new era is not as temperate as had been forecast
by glaciologists. Entire valleys and plains
remain under the Glacier's remnants,
still of impressive dimensions even though
its bulk is enormously reduced.
Nor did the cleared spaces ascend to their prior elevation

as quickly as predicted
once the weight of the Glacier was removed
—which causes problems with drainage:
extensive swamps have developed in some regions
while others suffer from
a lack of irrigation water.
Gigantic moraines of rock
mark the farthest points reached by the Glacier.
Not only are these miniature mountain ranges
an impediment to the construction of rail and road links.
But due to a curious grinding effect of the retreating ice,
many of the boulders' jagged edges have been honed sharp enough
to significantly injure anyone who has the misfortune to stumble
scrabbling through the blockage on foot.

Worse is the unaccountable persistence
of icy wind through the world.
New eddies and currents have somewhat altered
the relentless flow
yet the surges of chill air seem as slow to dissipate
as landforms to resume their former altitudes.
This apparition from the expanses
once the preserve of the Glacier
swirls about the avenues where picketers and parades denounce
the continued influence of the ice. And the wind
circles without pause the buildings
in which scientists and government officials meet to assign priorities
and mobilize all under their command
to inaugurate, they insist, an era of beneficence and calm.

OUTRIDER

Solitary first riders advance into legend.
—Robert Duncan, the "Pindar" poem

Not first riders, we journeyed for many years with the tribe
performed the songs they listened to and sang
crafted the art they displayed and circulated among themselves
fabricated the adornments they bore

When the caravan's route veered
from its former direction
some of us who had embellished the group's struggles and joys
withdrew to ride alone

flanking the column now bright and noisy with
new banners, sounds, accoutrements
meant to prefigure the tribe's altered destination
—all garish, discordant, ostentatious

to those of us who form a thin screen at the main body's edge
faithful to our compatriots' earlier dreams
and who remain convinced that only where we were previously headed
could a nation be fashioned richer in rewards, more just in its administration

Yet each day the distance increases
from the place we believed we would travel together
At night, we who shadow the passage
of the vehicles and animals of the majority

keep to our own fires,
or when we gather in small groups
speak of strange activities
reported from the main encampment

"We were a better people
before," our abandoned handful sigh
telling each other we are not a conscience
but a presence

so if anyone's eyes lift amid the dust and racket of the cavalcade
they can see at the margins
a shifting horizon of men and women
who carry a different history of their lives

than that recited at assemblies currently
who bear tools and weapons that to the young are
odd-shaped and unfamiliar, who consult maps that detail
territory the priests and leaders

scoff at during official ceremonies
To anybody viewing from far off
the people's traverse of plains and wooded uplands
the circling outriders might appear

like herders, guiding and prodding the mass
But we separated ones
are only custodians of an alternative
discarded for the present

preservers and shapers of
uninstituted truths
oracles keeping up, keeping pace
singers of another road

BEATING

Passing close below joists, the skull
can take a shot as a dark surge, then
pain flare. Now, the left side of my face
receives the edge of a fist's
four-by-four post
igniting the almost-audible black flame.
Another four-by-four's butt end
crushes the ridge
over my right eye, third and fourth beams knock away
my raised forearms so a swarm of posts
thunder down a roil of agony,
my chin jerked to one side
on its bloody pivot. A huge spoon
from nowhere excavates stomach's
bladder of air to
no breath, no breath, each unbroken
no breath skin pore awash. Asphalt
jolts up to slam
my right shoulder. *Breath.* Metal bars,
their tips incandescent, slash
into spine, back,
pestle
after pestle
hammers into my ribs, left knee.
Through gaps in the smoke
I glimpse grass tufts, house door
until a splintery wooden cone is jammed
down my windpipe, tight.
On a hot day, the surface of a lake
closes above me with a click
as my arms pull me
lower, breath held, supported and resisted

by fluid coolness
bounded with a layer of
ice.

MOVING ON

Okay, so I had an affair.
I prefer to think of it
as having been temporarily led astray by my feelings
for a woman I met through work
at a time when you and I
were experiencing difficulties in our marriage.
I realize what I did was hurtful to you.
But that's history.
I made an error. I've accepted the blame.
We need to move on.

    I admit I broke into the parking garage
    and hammered in a few car windows.
    I didn't have enough money
    and that was the only way
    I could get stuff to sell. I never meant
    to attack that couple: they were just in the wrong place
    at the wrong time. Can happen to anybody.
    I know what I did was definitely out of line.
    I told the judge I regret the trouble I caused.
    But I can't spend the rest of my life
    saying "Sorry." I've got to move on.

It appears that during the past year
out of hundreds of government contracts issued under my auspices,
in a single case
the recipient was a relative of mine.
I bear the entire responsibility.
Yet as I have repeatedly said,
the moment this situation was brought to my attention
I tracked down the source of this unfortunate occurrence
to an overzealous employee

who has since been let go. And I want to assure everyone
measures have already been adopted
to make certain this never takes place again.
I hope this isolated slip does not besmirch the reputation
of either my colleagues or myself.
Now that this incident is closed
we should all move on.

We in the industry recognize
that due to previously authorized practices
the resource that we all depend on has been depleted
to a temporarily unsustainable level.
Resource management, though, is a complex undertaking
while hindsight is cheap and easy
compared to operating a business which provides
a livelihood for thousands of our employees
and which also must meet the requirements of our shareholders.
As we enter this period of adjustment, we are confident
we are ideally positioned to move forward from here.

A few controversial studies can be interpreted
to suggest the world's supply of uncontaminated water
and air is falling below levels
necessary for the continued health of our species.
Some special interest groups believe
that fossil fuel consumption
has resulted in emissions which have altered
global climatic zones, allegedly shrinking food production
and threatening widespread displacement not only of people
but also plants and wild creatures,
many of which may fail to thrive under new conditions.
Yet if there is one characteristic
for which humans are rightly famed

it is our ability to learn from our setbacks.
Should we ever reach the point
where this planet has been rendered uninhabitable,
we can't let even a problem as serious as this
overshadow our species' tremendous achievements.
We'll just have to put the past behind us
and move on.

AUTUMN FIRES

Golden aspen and alder
explode against spruce on the mountains
and along the shrunken rivers,
feathery larches flare yellow-orange
between the pines

as in the valleys, smoke drifts:
water-smoke where slopes and ridges exhale
after the chill rain,
also denser plumes that pulse upward
from hillside and village
as flames consume slash,
prunings,
leaves.

Sparks ignited from rock
are no older than those
from diesel and match. Beasts
swarm in the dark
beyond the beasts seated around the fire.
In the flickering glare
hands fashion weapons,
rakes, cradles,
gods. Bright eyes meet eyes
as another branch is hauled
to the blaze.

        At dawn
a cottonwood thirty feet high

flaunts its glory,
incandescent as a fire equally huge.

Yet somebody studied flame,
grasped it could be sown.
Thus, tents burn,
corn ricks,
hootches. And the great barns
that house others' gods:
the towers of Jerusalem,
Lindisfarne,
of Barcelona, Munich,
Washington.

Pillars of darkness
and of fire,
prayers, banners, laboratories
hope to invoke the beauty promised
around the curve of the planet,
from aphelion to perihelion
to aphelion again. Below decks
chained prisoners with a stolen flint
set the vessel alight,
while above, the ship's naturalist
maps at the glow of a lamp
the circulatory system of a strange fish.
In his hammock, the gunner dreams of a shell
to bring down an entire mast.

Autumn by autumn,
flames rage
to rid the earth of dross
so what ensues may flourish.
We have only the lifespan of a star
to get it right.

GYPSY HIGHWAY

BALLAD OF THE WINDSHIELD WIPERS

The light was frozen

        Ay!

Below a curtain of living rock and snow
Borealis of mountain blocking the horizon
A car crosses
A white field

        Ay!

Now the horses are circling
Around the halted vehicle
They lean over the fire
Of its hood
Their lips are icy steam

Later, tracks
Uncurl through the black snow
Whispers of flakes
Hang in a rigid cube of air
The blades of the wipers
Fly toward the bitter stars
Tooth marks on the beams of light

        Ay, the horses!

BALLAD OF DEATH AND THE GYPSY

Death is a gravel shadow
Beside the highway

A black deer
Poised
Among roadside crosses

That mark its territory
Haunch of an elk
Suddenly transcending the windshield
Without sound:
A hide
Of death

Death is afraid of beauty
That is why it kills

The gypsies say
If you die behind the wheel
You forever drive a route
Where sunspray splinters into
Leaves of birch and aspen
On a curve that draws toward easy hills
Meadow and the empty range
Just greening, the pavement
Empty far as an eye reaches
Engine steady

But death
Brays its hoofed laugh
At this, turns
The tunnels of its eyes

Toward you, from the shoulder
In the lights approaching, says

>   *Toll*
> *To pay*

BALLAD OF THE BROTHERHOOD

Canyon of rock
           And hemlock
Sing through the snow

           B-train
Flashes its lights
Gears descending, gypsy leans from a high window
                        Wreck ahead

Cab become a cliff of ice
Wraiths on the road
           Gesture
Slow, slow

          Trailer
On its side, the terrible
Underbelly
        exposed

BALLAD OF THE ROAD

the road is one long tune: three guitar notes
in sequence, then a chord
and the sequence repeated.
a harp starts to groan and buzz,
also driving the highway forward,
the chord changing as the road
slopes downgrade
and slows for a turn
while a sax takes the asphalt over a river.
behind the relentless progression of struck strings,
drums and bass
—harmony's tires and engine—
pulse in the sternum, the belly.

the road is a songline
that crosses uplands, then
nudges into a valley town,
pauses for a light
and at the outskirts again
accelerates back to a fast tempo.
the songline is owned by
everyone: we die
but the road twists toward the horizon,
refrain and key intact,
streaming into another year without us
like a black flood, a party
that doesn't stop, a flute trill
that names the misty weather
above on a mountain's face,
a wind that rocks the vehicle
approaching the summit, chorus of wheels
never still, never silent: living artery of the land

that names us,
sings us here, sings us on.

GYPSY HIGHWAY

Road and its weather
Roses for the mind

A love-dream: thought
Finally free of its body

Water shaped by the land
Confined to a channel

Pooling at an obstruction
Released

To erode a cutbank
Ascend a mountain

Drown the stones of rapids
Meander

When I evaporate
The road will not mourn

I will fall again to earth
A wind

Singing the distances
A dream

To the end of
Weather

A RING WITHOUT A STONE

Who transplanted the first geranium?
Who baked the first bread?

When I touched her hand
I was not thinking of my mother, nor she of hers.

Her sudden kisses, the sweetness she murmured:
How could these arise, and from where?

Could someone love
a man of confusion and single-mindedness?

We slipped away toward the river.
Somewhere a bell, another bell, a rooster.

EYE BALLAD

She gave me her name and her hand
The café quieted

                But what I saw
were the green discs

she peered through, beautifully pale
as the underside of birch leaves

or a glacier-fed river
flowing below a high cirque

If the strings of my guitar
had eyes

they would be this slight green, the hue
of the eyes of death

                She strode
past me to the street

leaving her eyes
pale, pale

the birch leaves
the water

ANTI-MOTHER BALLAD

Long live Death
—Falange Española Tradicionalista
slogan, 1936

The young women
fussing with satchels of gear, with strollers,
awed and full of self-praise at
the accomplishment of their bodies,

at a task they watched, abetted,
then achieved with great pain: another helpless being
brought to term. The mothers
in their smug innocence

provide the sweetness of milk,
the comfort of dry, of warm noises
and softness, the knowledge
that these delights will vanish:

these mothers give birth
to death—*death*
in its baptismal gown
death on its tricycle

death taken hand-in-hand to a
first day of school
death who stares at
mewling, crawling kittens

now still: the shock that
death, too
is to die
Death discovering

in the anecdotes of its peers
the anatomy of the other accomplice
to death, sudden
alterations to death's body

to prepare it for death, the living dead
speak about a book that claims
death has been rescinded
for some, death

in love, death making
the death from which
emerges
the blessing

GYPSY LOVE

After four kids, she told me,
all breast-fed, I don't feel a thing
there
anymore. I took my lips from a nipple.
They sucked everything out, her voice shrugged.
You're wasting your time. Her laugh said,
That's how it is. I heard
my boots compress the gravel
as I walked the highway shoulder.
Cars, trucks speeding by, moving someplace.
Her legs and arms
squeezed around me.

EMPLOYMENT APPLICATION

Mountains fill my eyes
The lift of a slope of evergreens
interrupted by a grey cliff that
the verdant flow encircles
and rises past
as, down here, I inhale
the sour odour of
rain on dry asphalt
—a scent dense as a mown hayfield's

Five months in an auto parts warehouse, three
in a tire dealership, six weeks on a roadside
brushing contract
Also shoulder bottle and can collecting, and, yes
asking for gas money in a parking lot
A week driving tractor with a bailer

Such hours, days are my prisons
But my work is
hauling in vistas of
heavy white mist that blurs the summits
—a cloud whose trailing tattered edges
mean rain on the forest uplands
and snow, this season, in the highest passes

where I cross a ridge and descend
toward spring, slabs of stone in the cuts
topped with caps of moss

This land so huge
one can never see enough of it

New colts shadowing the mares
in the greening pasture
Calves among the herd that stands
between unmelted drifts on a hillside

Three months in cab trim, a day
as a barista, most of a course in
small engine repair, labourer
on a cement crew

ROAD REPORT

Tattered shreds of snow
    batter the open phone booth
deafened by flaps of wind

Faint gypsy voice
in one ear
The pass is shut
due to snow squalls
You are going
nowhere

    B-trains, C-trains
and single axles
jake down past the
gas pumps, ignoring Highways'
Road Closed Ahead
A crow skitters atop the sleet
A coal freight
shrieks and rattles its empties
upgrade

    Even the gypsy's glacial laugh
is moving

WAVE

THE CAPE

A boy gallops across the yard of a ranch house
through the clouded morning,
a long cape trailing from his neck

                  and at the wheel
of my truck that powers by
I sense tight against my windpipe
the collar of a red corduroy rectangle: faded living-room drapes
my mother transformed on her Singer
so I could dash over the lawn
and swing off the porch,
a prince or musketeer.

                The hero I was,
the boy I glimpse,
prance with the weight of honour, of nobility
that flows behind, or swirls to
wrap a carapace of command
around shoulders.

Now after me streams
exhaust, a train of
pavement. I cover ground slumped in a seat, faster
than any child can race, my neck
cashiered, stripped
of an enduring
splendour.

WIND CAROL: THE WEIGHT

The gale all night wrapped its arms around the house
and shook it: the storm's desire
was to uproot the building, tug it free of the ground,
spin it like a leaf.

                In a dark bedroom
I thought how I have moved through my life
like wind: a swimmer who must propel himself
or drown.

            As a child,
I perceived I had been thrown into water
over my head.
I thrashed arms, legs
until I clumsily impelled myself
out along prescribed channels toward the sea.
I knew nothing of a safe destination, harbour,
only this necessity for
propulsion

                as the wind
must flow or perish. Tree branches try to flag it down:
"Rest here," they sigh
or whistle, but wind knows
to roost is death.

            When love
encountered me while I plunged ahead
I believed love would be a weight
clutching me, hauling me
under. I determined

to swim *with* love
but not to let it affix itself.

Words, too
—all I said and fought for—
were pushed before me like ripples,
a bow wave
circling about me, passing astern.
To find the words deepest within
was impossible, a passage in the wrong direction:
if my motion forward ceased
I would sink
just how gusts
build only windrows
where the detritus swept before the storm, or worn away,
stacks up in sculpted mounds.
"Artistic," some call the shapes
but the wind has already departed,
riffling the ocean's surface
in beautiful fan-shaped patterns
that pulse outward and vanish
forever

while underneath,
the immense mass of the sea
is heaved in long swells
of unstoppable energy, shifted by a power
greater than the earth itself,
a force that causes even a star
to spin and travel, accompanied by its planets
whose moons also swim effortlessly through the blackness
between the wheeling myriads of suns.

SNOW MAN

With my snowscoop, I push
mounds of white between myself and you

clearing a space for me to live, while the heaped snow
forms an obstruction low enough to talk across

but high enough to be a barrier. In every season
the rasp of my push-shovel against concrete

shifts away the frozen water
—beautiful in its minutiae, treacherous

and isolating en masse—to reinforce a wall
that lets me breathe, offers the chill solace

of empty room, occupied only by
what could grow, or be built, here

if the snow ever stops.

SILENCE

The fury, lust, hate
I can not utter
condense on the sides of my throat
from the air that flows by my vocal cords
wafting the syllables I am able to articulate
past my teeth.

Such globules that coat my larynx
sparkle with bitter acid
as they streak the walls of my gullet
to pool in the stomach:
a roiling cauldron
no one but myself visits.

When I peer through the vapour
rising from that tub, I see my bodily shell
shattered, fragments
dissolved, my being become
a single deep-pitched yowl
coated with poisonous dark fur

and fanged, bulked with the power
filtered out of what I manage to speak,
its roar silencing an entire valley,
flattening trees, furrowing the ground
in an avalanche track:
myself brought at last before the world

and not caring.
They will have to burn me
because if I am interred
nothing will grow on that site for a thousand years.

BALLAD OF THE DESTROYED GUITAR

Her absence poured damp stones
into the open "O"
of my guitar, the box's bottom
warping, bulging as more rocks thundered in

until the thin wood sagged free
from the instrument's sides
revealing little steel
needles, that had secured the device

many years ago, when the glue first set.
I hoisted the splintered machine
to my waist, the guitar with its stones almost heavier now
than I could heft

and strummed. As my fingers
plucked each string in turn, it snapped
except one, which continues to utter
the hum of a river,

of the plod of boots
on the dust of a track in the moonlight
crossing hilly country, perhaps a desert,
the milestones and signposts

defaced, rotted off, pulled face down in the gravel,
past which thrum the irregular rhythm of the hoofs
of the pack horse I tug after me
laden with panniers and boxes

stuffed with discarded knives,
chips of glass and tile, rusted muffler piping
—the hitches I tied giving way, the animal's burden
slipping, askew, above the empty road.

LOVE LOSS BALLAD

I stand yet again in the self-serve to pump
into the tank
a damaged, an assassinated love and
steer away

Hour by hour, hayfield and then
forest
shafts and axles spun steady by *how could she say*
and *I should try*

Summitting the pass into drier air
while huge white
mountains float in the blue: *how will I ever*
Maybe her

compressed, vapourized, ignited
and exploded
in each piston according to the
tuning

that causes the odometer, ranges, the morning
to turn
and turn once more, switchbacking the long route
up from the lake town

over the ridge and down into
basin
the convulsive starkness of loss
hammering

so rapidly, implacably, the motor and radials
blend
to a steady note
—solid

centre line, black shoulder, *she*, oh, *passing lane*

COMPANION

Taller than me by a head, more burly
Each time I encounter him he insists
on proffering his hand
though I know what's coming: his grip
a car door that slams on my fingers
In my agony, I try not to flinch
as he keeps his expression neutral, mocks
Really great *to see you*
I always intend to apply equal pressure
Yet in his grasp my muscles wither, turn
ineffectual
We remain frozen in this posture
until he tires of the game
Hours thereafter spent around him
are organized to his
liking—meals are served when he hungers, and
he decrees the menu

How can you stay friends
with such a bully, other friends demand
But we first met when as a child
I inched across a log above a mountain torrent
and observed my companions witness my fate
with empty stares
He accompanied me amid crowds yelling on the street
under the massed clubs of the police
and on occasions across a table or bed
I had to speak unpronounceable, unbearable words

He remains present during every instance
the jet I travel aboard abruptly banks
to drop, uncontrolled, five miles

to earth, and also when from the line of traffic racing toward me
a car too near emerges into my lane
He shares the repeated sessions
where I count and recount my years left before
whoever I am stops savouring
the light that vibrates through the aspen leaves

After these decades, moreover, I am familiar with his oddities
—his fascination with photos of the dead, with
tattoos, discordant music
Plus, his kindnesses
—his belief his rough approach assists me
to face what I abhor

And he is the one who will walk beside me
when I have to voyage
alone into the dark

NEARER TO THE SUN

COYOTE WIND

No place Coyote doesn't stick
his cool damp nose. When he comes to town
                              he's a blustery night
tipping garbage cans
                    and spreading scraps of plastic, old credit card receipts,
bits of electrical tape.
He knocks over bird feeders
                      and hanging flower baskets
as well as rattling a few doorknobs
in case somebody's house is unlocked.
He can sniff out mischief
he might get to inside.

Coyote's a magician:
                    cats and dogs vanish
whenever he gusts by. The moment trees are in leaf
in spring, he starts their branches waving
and hardly stops. By September
the tree is so worn down from all that motion, its leaves
dry out, begin to change colour.

                    Some say
Coyote is responsible for the spike in gasoline prices.
                    Some say
he has a paw in the disappearance of the ozone.
        Some say
if you're unemployed it's because the more places Coyote is spotted
the less jobs there are.

                    Coyote won't hang around
to refute such charges. He's already jogging toward

the next settlement, tongue lolling,
his breath causing blowdowns in the woods,

                                                        gales at sea,

dangerous crosswinds on the highway
and kites
to soar high over the hill
and hold steady up there
as his huge, airy grin.

NOCTURNE III

The cat by the stoop
has conjured wind
streaming through the weeping birch and
spruce trees. Her eyes
have formed the world
of blacks and greys
and the street lamp shaking in the gale.
If the cat could
she would fashion a brown moon
beaming onto an orange lawn. Instead,
she creates shadows of shadows.
At this moment, she also concentrates on
fending away drops of water
amid the tumult of air.
Night, the cat commands,
remain fierce, dark,
dry.

CALGARY

A slag heap of dollars
with portions hidden behind facades
designed by famous international architects
down on their luck
—an immense tailings mound of money
toward which fleets of tanker trucks
sloshed full of additional cash
stream to disgorge

Two inches of fresh snow overnight
at mid-May

A buffalo standing, head lowered, defeated
as though formed of suburban ornamental brush
in a yard beside the traffic stalled at the corner of
32nd Avenue and Shaganappi
just east of Market Mall

                    Cigarette smoke
churning onto the street from the bar doorways
where according to the police crime tally
young white men stab each other every second midnight
alternating with Vietnamese gangs whose preference for disputes is
pistols and long guns

                    A metropolis in which
nobody is born
permitting the demolition of half the hospitals
and the resultant tax saving applied
to subsidize private plastic surgery clinics

                                        A blizzard
pushing southward in June, that drags down
limbs of the ornamental cherry
and suffocates the narcissus

                            A Dodge pickup
hauling two dead cows, heads lolling out the tailgate
in an attempt to hold at a distance
the customary flock of spoiler-equipped sports cars
quivering inches behind whatever moves along asphalt
in their anxiety to be anyplace else

                            Frost on the lawns
one July morning

                    Sour gas corporation CEOs
awarded annual remuneration
four hundred times the average wage of company employees
who still insist they are generously paid
A person who lives off investments
complaining about the sloth of the poor

                                Icy wind from the mountains
August 13th, snowflakes suspended in mid-air
from an overcast, melting when they eventually descend

Swaths of tract houses eating the Prairie
at each cardinal point: acres of treeless bloated dwellings
that seep outward from the shopping centres

                                        Sleet
in early September, the streets whitening

as the Bow River curls quietly through

wafting its suicides and abandoned mattresses
toward Hudson's Bay, lower trunks of the cottonwood
and aspen that line its route
wrapped in wire to discourage the presence of beaver
and thus demonstrate efficient management of the biosphere

To the north, the featureless hump of Nose Hill Park
rears over its expanding ring of freeways
—bleak tombstone for what failed to thrive

WINDFARM

West of Fort Macleod, where Highway 3
twists through the Foothills toward the Crowsnest Pass
row upon row of huge metal pillars
have been erected on the ridgelines, or rise individually
in a hay meadow or ploughed field: each column
topped with three immense blades
of a spinning propeller easily a third as large
as the shafts hoisting them into the air.

Official sources declare these are industrial windmills
for generating electricity. But nowhere is a power switchyard
or transmission tower visible.
Perhaps these twirling structures
are a clandestine regional project to draw moist Pacific clouds
inland across the Rockies, a scheme designed to end
years of drought in this area
where the irrigation reservoirs are empty by summer
and the river courses are at best thin creeks, if not muddy patches
at the bottom of the coulees.

Or maybe the devices
are an attempt to ameliorate a so-far-secret effect
of the warming biosphere: the slowing of the planet's rotation
as its atmosphere thickens with carbon dioxide, methane, fluorocarbons.
The resultant increase in the lengths of day and night
is predicted to impair crop growth
in every climate. Rather than alarm the population, governments
have constructed in out-of-the way corners
these revolving propellers intended to pull the earth forward
to stabilize its rate of turning:
pacemakers for an ailing world.

ABSENTIA

Et in Absentia ego

More remote than Nepal,
the country is so heavily treed
an observer who approaches its borders
would be forgiven for imagining unbroken forest
covers all except the rock faces and summits
of the highest peaks.
But the single road that winds
past a customs post, through valleys and across ridges
leads to hamlets, farms and small cities
housing a modestly industrious population.

The surprising characteristic of these municipalities
is a rural quiet that seems to mute
bustling thoroughfares.
In residential districts, an even denser silence
hums in the ears. Birds, vehicles, lawn mowers
produce their expected noises.
The sum of these, however—perhaps due to
the acoustical properties of the native conifers—
results in a lower decibel rating
than any suburban area's on the globe.

Yet social organization does not depart
from models most tourists could recognize:
providers of services are no more or less effective
or compassionate. Families run the gamut
from close to diffuse. Only jurisprudence here
is of special note, indeed has earned proverbial status,
for its practice of excusing the defendant
from participation in the legal process

—an approach which has caused other jurisdictions
to decline to recognize the validity of these courts,
in particular with regard to their own nationals.

Notwithstanding this legal anomaly
the place radiates a romantic attractiveness
to restless young people
or adults with an inability to form
meaningful relationships.
Also drawn to these precincts are individuals
whose behaviour exceeds their society's norms,
and wanderers possessed by the unquenchable urge to travel.
Men and women who stay for a few months
are not much influenced by the local milieu.
Yet newcomers who find employment, marry, raise children,
despite retaining for a while aspects of their original culture,
within a decade cannot be distinguished from
the other citizens of this state.

VOYAGE

On the promontory, the wind
fluttered and tugged our clothing
where we stood in a constant roar
as of the waves breaking on rocks
below the field. Like our hosts had mentioned
if we held our arms a little distance from our bodies
the stream of air on this sea-bright morning
was powerful enough to lift us
from our feet
and transport us three or four metres ahead
in an ungainly leap resembling astronauts
on the moon.
Such shouts of startled joy.
I watched a couple of my companions
ascend nearly vertically like a kite
and, steeling myself,
followed them up to where,
exhilarated and anxious,
I was suspended above the island
close to the tip of the metal flagpole
whose empty cables clanged in the light.
Here, I felt as when I have swum into water
greatly beyond my depth, amazed by my skill
but possessed of a swelling fear I might tire
or cramp, and drown. At these moments
I turn and stroke toward shore
—castigating myself when my feet touch sand
that I lost trust, did not remain longer
buoyed over nothingness.
From aloft, too, I swung quickly down
to land, buffeted by the gusts.

Then I took a steadying breath
and reascended until
—the whitecaps only specks, the entire shape
of the island visible on my right—
I float, thrilled and
frightened I will not be able to control
my eventual descent toward that patch of soil
but will plummet into sea. Mid-air,
the sound of waves
and the wind is muted
this much nearer to the sun.

YOUNG CLAUS

Claus as a junior executive
proved a *wunderkind*
yet his grades in his MBA courses
were definitely middle of the pack.
At twenty-nine he was a CEO
and this was long before dot-coms, remember.
He started in retail shoes
—unsexy as that sounds—
then he was in air freight
where he met the first Mrs. C.
He turned forty in financials
but niche—pensions, annuities,
every sort of product aimed at the aging or retired.

After forty he began to read
even in his office. I'd go in with a report
and he'd be deep in Plato or *War and Peace*.
He took a couple of Humanities courses, though oddly enough
at the local art school.
His second wife was a classmate
and into weird stuff. They spent the honeymoon
at that place in Scotland
where there's supposed to be elves
at the foot of the garden.
Then they were over in Finland
to visit the bunch who herd reindeer
—used to be called Lapps, except they have a politically correct name
nowadays. These guys were supposed to be big on
gnomes or trolls or suchlike.

None of this changed Claus' business sense, however.
He gets off the plane from Helsinki and walks into

a hostile takeover bid. When the smoke cleared
the company was stronger than before
with an influx of new capitalization
and we began to diversify. We even acquired
a toy company he expanded into a franchise chain
almost without paying attention. One of the directors of that outfit
was Mrs. Claus number three.
She wasn't lower mileage, either:
same age as him, in fact.
Around this time he got interested
—maybe it was her influence—
in what years later got termed ecology.
He'd bore me on the golf links about some scientists
who claimed to have detected
big temperature changes in the Arctic.
But the newest Mrs. C.'s main thing was karma:
why are some people rich and others poor?
Needless to say, if you'd snagged a guy worth nearly a billion
who was married, when you met him, to a knockout blonde kook
while you were okay-looking but
not even close to what's on the covers of supermarket magazines,
not to mention being in your early fifties,
I guess you'd be fascinated by life's little twists and turns, too.
Claus would muse on this philosophy gunk
by the hour, even in the middle of a strategy session
if I didn't turn the subject to some corporate problem
I knew he'd find temporarily more absorbing.
As best I grasped his line of thought,
he was trying to determine whether the link between
good or bad annual performance
and the material success or failure of a firm
had any parallel in personal behaviour.

When he turned sixty, he was still so full of beans

nobody was even whispering about succession.
Then one day he quits.
At the press conference, he spouts on vaguely
about the North as an untapped opportunity for enterprise
and that he feels he needs to pull the threads of his life together.
Of course, the rest
is old news.

THE LONELINESS OF BEAUTY

Orion burns in the southeast, rising
Over the valley rim up the evening sky.
Myth after myth, a man or woman
Is translated into a constellation,
Such immortality a god or goddesses' reward.
Yet what could feel lonelier
Than to be separated cold lights
Ablaze in the blankness, a being diffused
Across incalculable distances,
More removed from earth
Than either sun or moon.

                           Orion's burden
Was beauty: not just his own
—Of which the poets speak—but that of Merope,
Her smile, her graceful limbs
The goal of his labours, unattained
—Her father envious of Orion's form, his prowess.
On her behalf, for years he
Stalked and faced the giant boar,
Bear, wild dog
Alone. Denied his love, he
Chose to serve the Lady of Wildness
—Herself a solitary beauty—
Until in her jealousy or capriciousness
She tracked him, shot
A silver arrow into his heart, lifted his body
Into the moon's dominion.

Isolation is inherent in loveliness.
Who could befriend

An ideal?
Those less perfect, less desirable
Show envy, awe, but especially
Avoidance; they elect to mate
With one beside whom they feel more ease,
Consanguinity. In vain do the beautiful plead
Their outside is a veil.
Those who court them
Possess frequently an ugliness of soul, an audacious wish
To trample, despoil what the suitors yearn for,
Can not obtain.

        In the plaintive harmonies
Of Renaissance airs, hymns, anthems
Is heard the sadness of this conundrum, is audible
The parti-coloured autumnal forest that surrounds
Our habitations, that crowds to the edges
Of our fields of hay and grain
Now stripped of their gifts.
How poignant these woods are:
The path between oaks and a yew grove
Strewn with the first of the season's leaves,
Some elm branches already barren
In the cooling afternoon. Even the choral
Refrains of this music
Radiate a melancholy seclusion:
We may cluster by a fire
In the drafty hall or cottage
But each of us sits or lies
Staring into the beautiful warmth of the flames
Alone.

DUO

Across a table, her words
Refashioned lamps, cloths, bowls,
Her hands tugging
Her hair backwards while she spoke.

Her conversation was a lens
That brought the shapes and edges
Of each item, of the room itself
To a clarity, a rich distinctiveness
Some music can provide:
Sharpening and deepening
What is touched or smelled or
Tasted, detail
Infused with delight, a high relief
Suddenly added to the world.

AND ME HAPPIEST BEHIND A WINDSHIELD

Rising on 5, a four-lane
south of the Thompson River,
the highway lifting toward some minor summit,
piney woods transforming to hillsides of fir
while rain becomes sleet then snow
that hovers in the air but
does not touch ground,
the white lines and roadside posts
draw me upward as
The Hollies' "Carrie Ann" pounds its ancient
exuberant
complaint: the singers' path to joy
balked once more by a loved one's
vicissitudes—her rejection, that devastating loss
subsumed in the triumphant
music, in the route's endless high-speed
climb
through the terrifying
wonder of living.

TAKE MY WORD

INVOCATION

Poems scribbled, keyed, re-crafted
and keyed again
while the sun thrusts in past the marigolds
at the east window as the clock shifts toward
the irrigation sprinklers' next time to be
moved, so I return to the desk
having not only hauled and connected hoses
over July grass, but en route
tied a sagging gladiolus stem
or plucked a few weeds among radish leaves
causing both soil and moisture to cling to fingers
that scurry across plastic lettered buttons:
may your words, whatever their intent, embrace and contain
this mountain earth, its sky
and the circling water, O poems.

BÖK

He speeds forward on foot, swift
as a syllable draped in black:
a meme in cycling shorts
but without a machine
or maybe leading a zebra. He is
a Rimbaud of the phoneme,
scanning, as he travels, a dictionary of a language
fashioned entirely of metal
or snow. Crowds along his route
gasp, pelt him with boutonnieres
and protractors, the occasional
cow-pie, applause, anything but money

which his promoters,
mute dwarves, attempt to solicit
by extending their caps imploringly
to the audience now dissolving after his passage.
The diminutive men and women, speechless,
hope to extract gold from his absence
by employing only their
eyes.

THE BEST

words hustle down over
slippery rocks in a white push
that spreads ledge to
ledge: the crests of
small rills that pour
over and between the stones,
the shelves, glisten as they
descend, pool,
flow on

or in a night of deep snow
the words stand
on a glitter of white field
under a moon burning
nearly full,
their pockets empty
of keys, knife,
no coat,
defenseless against
the chill air, a starlit beauty, joy
so huge
it borders fear

READING A BOOK OF FORTY-EIGHT POEMS,
NOT ONE OF WHICH I UNDERSTAND

1

Sounds taste good to a child's mind.
Bo-bo-bo, she repeats with satisfaction
For a quarter-hour. The poet's joy in these poems

May lie in the delight of capturing
The simultaneity of the brain's
Attention: scent of marigold,

The house low on sugar, a moment in a novel
Dipped into last night where one character
Remembers a saying of her mother's,

The viciousness of management's decision
About the schedule at work.
The thoughts I experience from the poet's words

Flock and hop and cluster: juncos and chickadees
Circling the feeder suspended from a lower branch
Of the fir—three birds peck at the spill on the lawn,

Two are perched swaying on the apparatus itself, dozens more
Flit from an ash to the fir to the thin stalks of
A young maple. *Fee-bee*, the birds call. *Tchet, tchet.*

2

Except, each idea is not one thing.
Some drag below them nets, or banks of hooks
That catch on the rocks or sunken logs and other debris

Deep down. When I try to lift them
They are ponderously heavy, weighted by
An esoteric awareness—mythic or scientific or doctrinal—

Of the universe, that alerts me to a comprehension
I didn't know I possess, or to a huge vacancy,
An ignorance. Sectors in my brain yearn to classify,

Arrange, identify a pattern. Another region questions
Is consciousness an electrically generated cancer
Intelligence developed beyond a certain level

Is susceptible to? Why do I fear the random
Out of which we begin?
The pleasure for me in these lines

Resembles the moon's resplendent light, that originates
Not in that sphere of rock and dust
But in a furnace millions of kilometres distant, and invisible.

GARDEN

The young poets charge
into the garden, each brandishing aloft
the flower they have grown.

They encounter dozens of elderly-appearing men and women
hunched over or kneeling at
plots and beds to tend

with antique implements
dull blooms on sickly stems.
The old do not look at the visitors.

The recent arrivals confer
together, despite having previously regarded many of each other
with contempt. They take possession of

a bank of fresh earth close to the entrance,
except for a handful who claim a grassy slope
interspersed with knapweed, mullein, oxeye daisy.

Each of the young poets
jams his or her gazania or portulaca into dirt
and steps back. They wait.

No sound of applause
reaches them. They gesture toward
their flower, to indicate its splendours.

The ancient gardeners
continue working.
Now some of the visitors

observe for the first time
the extent of the park,
how its manifold greens

with their varying heights, the myriad shapes and colours of petals
stretch to the crest of a distant rise
and farther. A few of the newcomers

sigh loudly, utter a derisive snort,
abandon their lobelia or salvia
and stomp over to an elder

weeding alyssum
and kick a stone into her patch. The most impetuous
trample through a bed, sometimes repeatedly,

knock over a low ornamental fence. After a while
they tire, march away, disappear beyond
the area's boundary hedges.

Silver tools begin to soothe
disturbed earth.
The majority of young persons

remain beside their dahlias, zinnias, petunias
in the hot sun,
hiss of a distant impulse sprinkler.

They start to compare more acutely
the beauty they have fashioned
to the pathetic effects of those here before them.

One or two approach where
an elder toils. Ask to borrow
a rake or trowel.

JOURNAL

Its poems flow with the relentlessness
of freeway traffic speeding through farm country:
declarative sentence after declarative
statement. The import of these lines
lifts to a pitch of wistful, tinge
of distress, leavened by the deployment of esoteric nouns
or verbs, an archaic part of speech.
Aloud, their sound
is a radio voice audible from
a different room, a soothing power lawn mower
down the block: Mmm-mm-mm Mmm
mmm Mm Mm mmm, nothing querulous,
indignant,
disturbed. Their topics
are the deleterious effect of memory, a reflective puddle on a leaf,
eradication of plant species better suited to this soil and climate
than bluegrasses and fescues.

Such writing
heaves a sigh of contentment, a pleasurable
regret, satisfying ennui.

Only a few pages
that convey translations
are charred at the edges or
have smooth surfaces blotched
or a cavity ripped open to allow cries
smothered by the surrounding paper stacks
to emerge, ring out, be free.

TAKE MY WORD FOR

A change
A spin
An alternate route to where you're going
A friend you haven't seen in years
What it's worth
Better or for worse
All you can
Fast relief of symptoms
Twenty-four-hour protection
A security deposit
Peace of mind
Authorized use only
Gospel
A sign

POEM LULLABY

Sleep, poems
yet unformed, I
have other work
on the world-ridge
and ask you to lie down
a while. At my door
I have welcomed
your brothers, aunts, cousins.
When you wake, you also
will receive
my joyful embrace, a roof
and walls out of the wind,
a feast of whatever sustenance
gladdens your hearts.
But now I need you
to rest.

A different life calls me
for a time. Nothing you offer
or contain will be lost
in your dark bed.
With you slumber
the thicket of oaks and cedars
shielding the nuthatch and chickadee
who blurt advice.
Also the gloomy prophecy
of the eagle
high on a limb above the river.
Your dream lands are wide,
poems, wide as a mind
and I thank you

even as you doze
for the crone who holds out
to those she chooses
the bear king's mask,
for the cloaked man
met on the road, face shadowed
below a cowl
while two ravens that float tree to tree
keep pace as he strides forward.

Sleep. I will be here
when you rouse
yourselves. Yours is
the lovesick doe, the salmon
of the brook
with her glittering leap.
Behind your closed eyes
swirl tales of
the hours shaped by
labour: the barley field
disked, the fir
planed, the steel rod tempered.

                              Sleep,
poems, until I
summon you. Or if I never come again
through the winter weather,
I swear someone else
will open your curtains to light,
lead you forth.
What I request is not banishment,
not exile, not
farewell. You and your burden

shall not vanish
nor lose your powers.
You remain forever the beginning
of the story,
the word drowsing in the stone.

ACKNOWLEDGEMENTS

With thanks to the editors and staff of the following journals and anthology in which poems here have appeared or been accepted for publication:

AlbertaViews: "The Stone"
Arc: "Calgary"
The Antigonish Review: "High Speed Through Shoaling Water," "Poem Lullaby"
Contemporary Verse 2: "Windfarm"
Event: "The Cape," "Death of the Grandmothers"
filling Station: "Reading a Book of Forty-eight Poems, Not One of Which I Understand"
Grain: "A Bird Made of Light," "Absentia," "Ballad of the Pickups," "Coyote Wind," "A Ring Without a Stone," "Wind Carol: The Sound"
Horsefly: "Grove"
Labor: Studies in Working Class History in the Americas: "Anthem"
The Malahat Review: "Autumn Fires," "Ballad of the Road"
The Minnesota Review: "Carrot"
The New Quarterly: "Ballad of the Windshield Wipers," "Employment Application," "Moving On"
Ontario Review: "Ballad of Death and the Gypsy," "Ballad of the Brotherhood," "Messages," "Postmodern 911," "Secrets of Winter," "Shift," "Springbomb," "Who"
Our Times: "Memories of the Glacier"
Poet Lore: "Greenup"

PRISM international: "Inguinal," "Take My Word For"

Queen's Quarterly: "Teaching English"

White Ink, ed. Rishma Dunlop (Toronto: Demeter, 2007): "Anti-Mother Ballad"

Windfall: "Emblem," "The People Who Used to Own This Place," "Portrait of Myself as a Cloud, or Natural Feature on the Valley Floor," "Wind Carol: Aspen"

Windsor Review: "Post," "Voyage"

OTHER BOOKS BY TOM WAYMAN

Collections of Poems

Waiting for Wayman (1973)

For and Against the Moon (1974)

Money and Rain (1975)

Free Time (1977)

A Planet Mostly Sea (1979)

Living on the Ground (1980)

Introducing Tom Wayman: Selected Poems 1973-80 (1980)

The Nobel Prize Acceptance Speech (1981)

Counting the Hours (1983)

The Face of Jack Munro (1986)

In a Small House on the Outskirts of Heaven (1989)

Did I Miss Anything?: Selected Poems 1973-1993 (1993)

The Astonishing Weight of the Dead (1994)

I'll Be Right Back: New and Selected Poems 1980-1996 (1997)

The Colours of the Forest (1999)

My Father's Cup (2002)

Anthologies

Beaton Abbot's Got the Contract: An Anthology of Working Poems (1974)

A Government Job at Last: An Anthology of Working Poems (1976)

Going for Coffee: Poetry on the Job (1987)

East of Main: An Anthology of Poems from East Vancouver (co-edited with Calvin Wharton, 1989)

Paperwork: Contemporary Poems from the Job (1991)

The Dominion of Love : An Anthology of Canadian Love Poems (2001)

Non-Fiction

Inside Job: Essays on the New Work Writing (1983)

A Country Not Considered: Canada, Culture, Work (1993)